A HEALTHY LIFE

Getting Sleep

by Kirsten Chang

T0021211

BLASTOFF! READERS

BELLWETHER MEDIA • MINNEAPOLIS, MN

Blastoff! Readers are carefully developed by literacy experts to build reading stamina and move students toward fluency by combining standards-based content with developmentally appropriate text.

Level 1 provides the most support through repetition of high-frequency words, light text, predictable sentence patterns, and strong visual support.

Level 2 offers early readers a bit more challenge through varied sentences, increased text load, and text-supportive special features.

Level 3 advances early-fluent readers toward fluency through increased text load, less reliance on photos, advancing concepts, longer sentences, and more complex special features.

★ **Blastoff! Universe**

Reading Level

Grade **K**

Grades **1–3**

Grade **4**

This edition first published in 2022 by Bellwether Media, Inc.

No part of this publication may be reproduced in whole or in part without written permission of the publisher. For information regarding permission, write to Bellwether Media, Inc., Attention: Permissions Department, 6012 Blue Circle Drive, Minnetonka, MN 55343.

Library of Congress Cataloging-in-Publication Data

Names: Chang, Kirsten, 1991- author.
Title: Getting sleep / Kirsten Chang.
Description: Minneapolis, MN : Bellwether Media, Inc., 2022. | Series: A healthy life | Includes bibliographical references and index. | Audience: Ages 5-8 | Audience: Grades K-1 | Summary: "Developed by literacy experts for students in kindergarten through grade three, this book introduces the benefits of getting sleep to young readers through leveled text and related photos"–Provided by publisher.
Identifiers: LCCN 2021041256 (print) | LCCN 2021041257 (ebook) | ISBN 9781644875797 (library binding) | ISBN 9781648346644 (paperback) | ISBN 9781648345906 (ebook)
Subjects: LCSH: Sleep–Juvenile literature. | Sleep–Physiological aspects–Juvenile literature.
Classification: LCC QP425 .C453 2022 (print) | LCC QP425 (ebook) | DDC 612.8/21–dc23
LC record available at https://lccn.loc.gov/2021041256
LC ebook record available at https://lccn.loc.gov/2021041257

Text copyright © 2022 by Bellwether Media, Inc. BLASTOFF! READERS and associated logos are trademarks and/or registered trademarks of Bellwether Media, Inc.

Editor: Rebecca Sabelko   Designer: Andrea Schneider

Printed in the United States of America, North Mankato, MN.

Table of **Contents**

Time for Bed!

Jack puts on pajamas.
He brushes his teeth.
He reads a book.
Time for bed!

Why Is Getting Sleep Important?

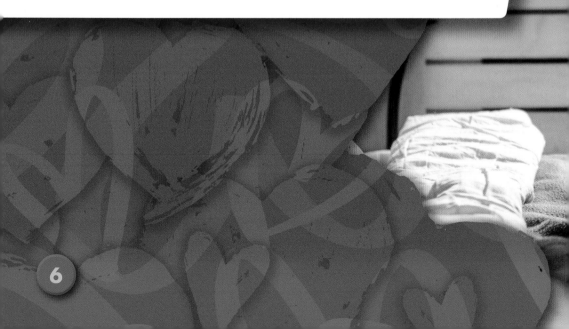

Getting sleep helps us stay healthy.

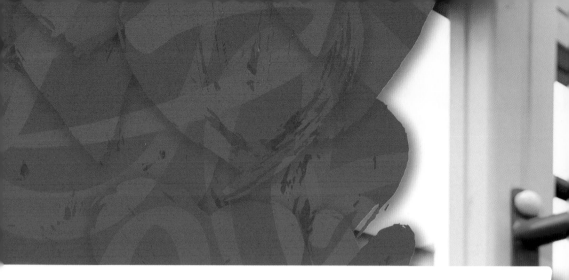

Sleep gives us **energy**. We use energy to play and learn.

Sleep helps the **brain** work at its best.
We think clearly.
We are **creative**.

Sleep improves our **mood**. We get along better with others when we sleep well.

How Does Getting Sleep Help?

more energy

think clearly

better mood

13

We may make
bad choices when
we do not sleep well.
We may get sick.

How Do We Get Sleep?

Ellie has a bedtime **routine** each night.

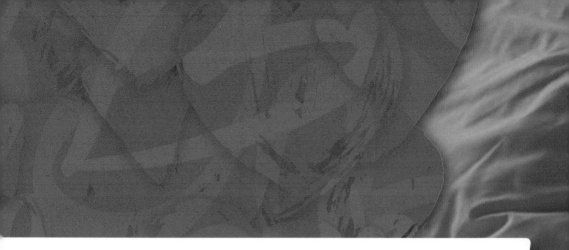

She puts on pajamas and reads a book. She sleeps in a dark, cool room.

Tools for Getting Sleep

bedtime routine

dark, cool room

no screens

Getting sleep is
an important part
of being healthy.
Good night!

Question

What is your bedtime routine?

Glossary

brain

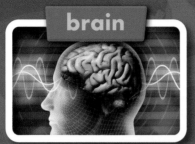

a body part inside the head that controls how you think, feel, and move

mood

the way you feel

creative

able to make new things and have new ideas

routine

something done in a certain order

energy

the power to be able to do things

To Learn More

AT THE LIBRARY

Black, Vanessa. *Sleep*. Minneapolis, Minn.: Jump!, 2017.

Chang, Kirsten. *Staying Active*. Minneapolis, Minn.: Bellwether Media, 2022.

MacReady, R. J. *Getting Enough Sleep*. New York, N.Y.: Cavendish Square Publishing, 2022.

ON THE WEB

FACTSURFER

Factsurfer.com gives you a safe, fun way to find more information.

1. Go to www.factsurfer.com.

2. Enter "getting sleep" into the search box and click 🔍.

3. Select your book cover to see a list of related content.

23

Index

The images in this book are reproduced through the courtesy of: LeManna, front cover (kid sleeping); Yuganov Konstantin, front cover (kid sleeping), pp. 6-7; Miyao, p. 3; Olesia Bilkei, pp. 4-5; Pressmaster, pp. 8-9; Ormalternative, pp. 10-11; anek.soowannaphoom, pp. 12-13; karelnoppe, p. 13 (more energy); Syda Productions, p. 13 (think clearly); ZouZou, p. 13 (better mood); ake1150sb, pp. 14-15; Lightfieldstudioprod, pp. 16-17, 18-19; Casezy idea, p. 19 (bedtime routine); Elena Chevalier, p. 19 (dark, cool room); Imgorthand/Getty, p. 19 (no screens); New Africa, pp. 20-21; Andreus, p. 22 (brain); SDI Productions, p. 22 (creative); FatCamera, p. 22 (energy); ESB Professional, p. 22 (mood); Lapina, p. 22 (routine); 19Thunvar, p. 23 (kid yawning).